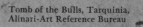
Tomb of the Bulls, Tarquinia,
Alinari-Art Reference Bureau

Amazon from the rim of an urn, bronze,
British Museum

Tomb of the Baron, Tarquinia, Alinari-Art Reference Bureau

# THE ART OF THE
# ETRUSCANS

by Shirley Glubok

*Designed by Gerard Nook*

*Special Photography by Alfred H. Tamarin*

HARPER & ROW, PUBLISHERS · NEW YORK, EVANSTON, AND LONDON

*The author gratefully acknowledges the assistance of:*
OTTO J. BRENDEL, Professor of Art History and Archaeology, Columbia University
MARGARET R. SCHERER, Former Research Associate, The Metropolitan Museum of Art
KATHARINE E. FLEMING, Chairman of Classes Six and Seven, The Chapin School
OLIVER PETTY, Chairman of Science Department, Patchogue-Medford School District
MASTER PETER LIPTON

*And especially the helpful cooperation of:*
ELAINE LOEFFLER, Department of Fine Arts, Brandeis University

*Other books by Shirley Glubok:*

THE ART OF ANCIENT EGYPT
THE ART OF LANDS IN THE BIBLE
THE ART OF ANCIENT GREECE
THE ART OF THE NORTH AMERICAN INDIAN
THE ART OF THE ESKIMO
THE ART OF ANCIENT ROME
THE ART OF AFRICA
ART AND ARCHAEOLOGY
THE ART OF ANCIENT PERU

*Front panel illustrations:*
Tomb of the Leopards, Tarquinia; Horseman, Tomb of the Baron, Tarquinia, photographs by Alfred H. Tamarin

*Back panel illustration:*
Tomb of the Baron, Tarquinia, photograph by Alfred H. Tamarin

An ancient legend tells that the people of Lydia, in Asia Minor, suffered a long famine. Food was so scarce that they had only enough for every other day. So they invented games—dice, knucklebones, and ball—to take their minds off their hunger on the days when they could not eat. But after eighteen years the famine grew even worse. Thus the king divided his people into two groups; one was to leave the country, and the other would remain. They drew lots, and the losers sailed far away to Italy where, according to the legend, they formed the Etruscan civilization.

Banqueter from the lid of a caldron, bronze,
The Metropolitan Museum of Art,
Fletcher Fund, 1927

In truth no one really knows where the Etruscans came from. About twenty-five hundred years ago, they were a rich and powerful nation in central Italy. At one time Rome was ruled by Etruscan kings. Later, the Romans conquered the Etruscans and destroyed their cities but not their cemeteries. These underground homes of the dead were often filled with art. We have come to know the world of the Etruscans through their art.

The Etruscans seem to have believed that when a man died, his soul

Tomb of the Augurs, Tarquinia, Anderson-Art Reference Bureau

lived on. They cut underground tombs out of the bedrock, and made them like the insides of their everyday homes. They filled them with everything the dead person might need in his afterlife.

Pictures were painted on the rock walls, showing funeral celebrations, dancing, feasting, and sports, as well as scenes from mythology and daily life. The painting at the left shows a wrestling contest. Paintings of a banquet scene are on the walls above.

These underground tombs were sealed off from the air. So the paint is astonishingly fresh, even after twenty-five hundred years.

Etruscan art very often looks Greek. The Etruscans admired Greek art. They sailed to the East to trade and brought home Greek masterpieces, and they invited Greek artists to set up workshops for them in Italy. Perhaps the subjects for these two paintings were taken from Greek mythology.

The paintings were made on large pieces of terracotta and placed on the walls of a tomb. Terracotta is baked clay.

In the painting on the left three people are walking. Each carries a different object. In the painting on the right a running man, holding a bow and arrows, is followed by a winged youth with winged heels, who carries a woman in his arms.

Colors for Etruscan paintings came from minerals and rocks. For example—chalk made white, oxidized iron made red, and charcoal made black.

Tomb of the Triclinium, Tarquinia Museum, Alinari-Art Reference Bureau

This gay, carefree dancer is from the wall of a tomb. A banquet scene was painted on one wall, with musicians and dancers on the walls at either side. The young man moves along with graceful rhythm. His short mantle, or cloak, seems to be swaying with his movement as he glides past the small trees.

The lovely face of a young woman on the right is also from a banquet scene. We know her name, Velia. It is written on the wall.

The face is beautifully drawn, with a noble profile and sad eyes.

Velia wears jewelry and a wreath of leaves in her hair. This picture is from a later period than the banquet scene.

Tomb paintings were made right on the rock walls. First the walls were smoothed and polished. Then plaster was usually spread over the walls. The figures were outlined by quick sketching strokes and filled in with color. When color is laid on while the plaster is still wet, the paint sinks into the wet plaster and lasts for a long time. Painting on wet plaster is called *fresco*.

Tomb of the Underworld, Tarquinia, Alinari-Art Reference Bureau

9

This life-size man and woman are on the lid of a sarcophagus. A sarcophagus is a large coffin.

The couple are resting together, married in death as they were in life. They lie side by side on a dining couch, the husband's arm around his wife. The couple seem part of a joyful feast. The Etruscan custom of allowing women to dine with men seemed strange in the ancient world.

The sarcophagus is made of terracotta, which is unusual, for it is difficult to bake such large clay objects. Etruscan artists loved to work with clay because it is soft and easily modeled.

Like most ancient statues, the figures were once brightly painted, but the paint has worn off.

Tarquinia Museum, Anderson-Art Reference Bureau

In earlier times Etruscans believed in cremating, or burning, the bodies of the dead and placing the ashes in urns called canopic jars. The terracotta urn on the left is topped by a figure that probably represents a dead person. The figures on the rim are men and women mourning for the dead man. The birdlike heads between

British Museum,
photograph by Alfred H. Tamarin

them are griffins, imaginary creatures.

Many small bronze containers were put in tombs as gifts to the dead. The vessel at left, with the long-necked animal heads, rests on four wheels.

The terracotta statue of a seated woman at right was found in a tomb with two other statues, another woman and a man. They probably represent the family of the dead person. Their right hands are outstretched as if to receive an offering. This woman wears large earrings and a cloak fastened at the shoulder by a clasp like a fancy safety pin.

The homes and temples of the Etruscans were made of wood or other light material. They have vanished. But some of the terracotta figures that decorated the temples have been saved. At the left is the head of a terracotta statue that probably stood on the roof of a temple. The Etruscans worshipped Greek gods, often giving them different names. This head may represent Zeus, king of all the gods. The curls on his forehead, his oval eyes, and his slight smile are in the style of the period known as *Archaic*.

Villa Giulia,
Alinari-Art Reference Bureau

Above is a terracotta *antefix,* an ornament that decorated the end of a tile roof. It represents a Gorgon, a monster from Greek mythology.

The Gorgon Medusa was once a beautiful maiden. She insulted the goddess Athena, who punished her by transforming her into a monster with hissing serpents for hair. She was so horrible that everyone who looked at her turned to stone. The hero Perseus cut off Medusa's head. He avoided looking directly at her by using his shining shield as a mirror.

Villa Giulia, Alinari-Art Reference Bureau

At the left is another antefix. It is in the form of a winged man with animal ears, whose feet turn into snakes.

The proud winged horses on the right also decorated a temple. They are modeled in *relief*. A relief is like a picture but the forms are raised and stand out from the background. The yokes around the horses' necks harnessed them to the chariot of a god. They seem to be ready to fly through the air, pulling their chariot. The relief is about four feet high, but it is so powerful that it seems larger. The horses were probably modeled in one piece, apart from the wings and tail.

The Etruscans were skilled horsemen. They bred horses for riding, racing, and pulling chariots.

The figure on the left represents the god Apollo, ready to spring at the hero Heracles. Heracles had tried to steal the holy hind, a doe with golden horns and hooves of brass. The animal was sacred to Apollo's sister Artemis, so the god was fighting for it.

The story was told in four life-size terracotta statues that stood out against the sky on the roof of a

Villa Giulia,
photograph by German Archaeological Institute, Rome

temple. Apollo's drapery clings to his body and falls in even folds.

A close-up of Apollo's head at the right clearly shows the large, slanting eyes and smiling lips of the Archaic style. It is indeed one of the great masterpieces of ancient art.

The statue was probably made in the workshop of Vulca of Veii, the only major Etruscan artist we know by name.

Below is a bronze chimaera—a fantastic beast with the body of a lion, a goat's head growing out of its back, and a serpent for a tail. This Etruscan statue was admired by an Italian artist, Benvenuto Cellini. He mended the chimaera's serpent-tail when the statue was nearly two thousand years old. Cellini lived about four hundred years ago.

An ancient legend tells about two baby boys, grandsons of a king. They had a

Archaeological Museum, Florence, Brogi-Art Reference Bureau

wicked great-uncle who stole their grandfather's throne, imprisoned their mother, and left the babies alone by the Tiber River to die. A she-wolf found them and nursed them. The boys, Romulus and Remus, grew up to be the founders of Rome, the great city on the Tiber River. The she-wolf became the symbol of Rome.

In Etruscan times this bronze she-wolf stood by itself. The two little boys were added around the time of Cellini.

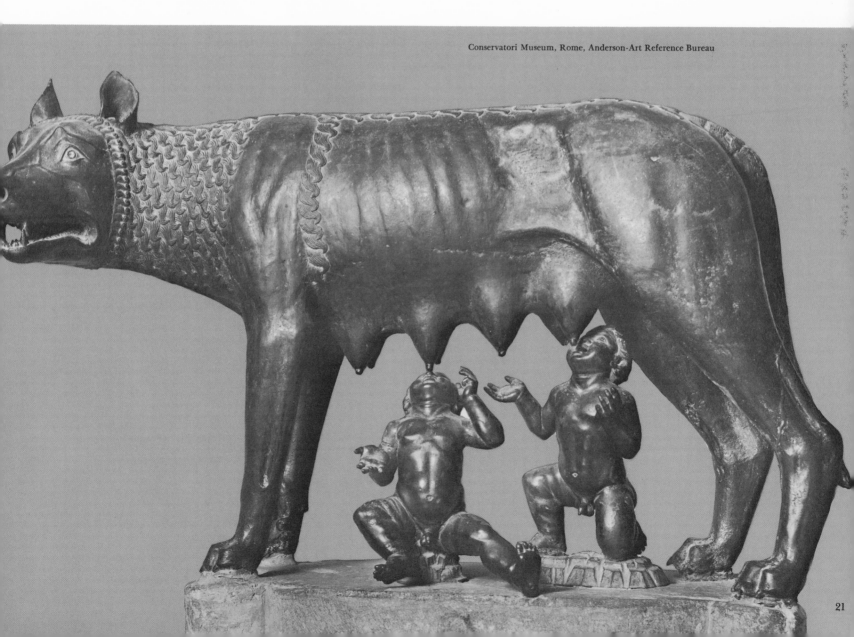

Conservatori Museum, Rome, Anderson-Art Reference Bureau

The Etruscans had plentiful copper and iron deposits, as well as tin and lead mines. They were master craftsmen in metal, especially bronze. Bronze is a mixture of minerals, mostly copper, with a small amount of tin.

This fine head of a boy is from a bronze portrait statue. A portrait is a likeness of a real person. The sad eyes and gentle mouth make the boy seem kind. The eyes were once inlaid with colored paste or stone. This portrait head is from a period later than the Archaic.

Archaeological Museum, Florence, Alinari-Art Reference Bureau

22

This bronze statue of a warrior wears a helmet with a high crest and cheek guards that are turned up. He wears body armor made of overlapping plates of metal. Under the armor he wears a tunic.

The body of this bronze warrior was formed in one piece, and the arms and shield were added afterward. The spear he once held has been lost.

British Museum, photograph by Alfred H. Tamarin

This chariot was found in the tomb of a warrior and may have been used just for his burial. It is made of wood covered with thin sheets of bronze.

The chariot is decorated with three scenes that may represent a myth about a warrior. The relief on the front shows the warrior receiving his armor from a woman, before starting off to battle. One of the side panels shows him driving a chariot drawn by a pair of winged horses. On the other side panel the warrior is fighting his enemies. At the right is a close-up view of that panel.

The Metropolitan Museum of Art,
Rogers Fund, 1903,
photograph by Alfred H. Tamarin

Louvre, Paris, Alinari-Art Reference Bureau

The Etruscans were brave warriors who excelled in their military deeds. These bronze warriors are fighting each other with daggers. The figures form the handle on the lid of a *cista,* a round box used by women to hold mirrors, combs, hairpins, and tweezers. Cistae were also used as urns for ashes in tombs.

The handle below is in the form of two soldiers carrying the body of a dead comrade. The dead soldier is very stiff; the others look quite alive, yet sad. The lid of the vessel to which they are attached can be seen.

Vatican Museum

The cista handle above is in the shape of two people riding on the backs of birds. They make a graceful pair, facing each other but leaning in opposite directions.

The mermaid at right looks as if she could slither through the water with ease. Her outstretched arms balance her arched fishtail. Her scales were made by engraving, or cutting into the surface of, the bronze.

Athletes were popular subjects for small bronze statues. At the right is a diver, just about to leap into the water. The youth's arms are extra long. They seem to be pulling him forward for his dive. Boxing, high jumping, discus throwing, horse racing, and chariot racing were other sports played by the Etruscans.

Munich Museum,
photograph by Walter Dräyer

Munich Museum, photograph by Walter Dräyer

29

This athlete is shown just as he is about to hurl his javelin.

The bronze acrobat below, doing a backbend, made a perfect handle for the lid of a cista. His feet and hands were attached to the lid, and his arched back was easily gripped.

The bronze figure in swinging motion is a *satyr*. Satyrs were mythological creatures who loved wine and music. Satyrs sometimes captured women and carried them off.

The Metropolitan Museum of Art,
Fletcher Fund, 1937,
photograph by Alfred H. Tamarin

The Metropolitan Museum of Art, Rogers Fund, 191
photograph by Alfred H. Tamar

Small bronze figures were formed by *solid casting*. First, an exact model of the object was made in wax and enclosed in a mold of clay. Next, the wax was melted out through holes that had been left in the clay, and the hollow space was filled with molten bronze. The mold was broken open to release the solid bronze figure. It was carefully polished, and finishing marks were cut into the surface with tools.

British Museum, photograph by Alfred H. Tamarin

At the left is the lid of a bowl showing Heracles wearing a lion's skin, with the horses of King Diomedes. A legend tells that Diomedes fed these horses on human flesh. They became so strong and spirited that bronze chains and iron stalls were needed to keep them under control. Heracles conquered them and fed Diomedes to his own horses.

The group of bronze figures below is on the lid of an urn for ashes. The handle is in the form of an athlete about to throw a discus. On the rim are four archers on horseback, holding their arms as if shooting arrows.

The Metropolitan Museum of Art,
Purchase, 1940, Joseph Pulitzer Bequest
photograph by Alfred H. Tamarin

This bronze dancing girl is holding an incense bowl on her head. She looks gay as she glides along, glancing back over her shoulder. Her huge hands and feet and her flowing robe make her seem all the merrier.

The Etruscans used the Greek alphabet, but they made different words with it. Modern scholars can read the words, but they do not yet understand what all of the words mean.

On the right is a clay pot in the shape of a rooster, with an alphabet of twenty-six letters. It starts out like the English alphabet, but many of the other letters are not the same, or they are in different order from the English ABC's.

The Etruscans left no books or written history. Most of the inscriptions that we have are from tombstones. The detail of the tombstone below shows Etruscan writing, which is written from right to left. (Greek is written from left to right.)

We can get an idea of the great wealth of Etruscan lords from the magnificent jewelry buried with the dead. This is one of the finest pieces of jewelry from the ancient world, a gold dress-pin about twelve and a half inches high. It was found in a grave of a princess. The top part has five lions in relief, and the bottom is decorated with winged lions and tiny ducks.

On the right is a gold pendant, an ornament that hung from a necklace. The photograph shows the pendant about six times bigger than its actual size. It is really only about an inch and a half high.

The head represents Achelous, a river god with horns and animal ears. Achelous' hair and beard are made of thousands of tiny grains of gold, by a method called granulation. Melted gold had to be formed into tiny balls, which were laid side by side on the surface, then joined together with molten metal. It was very difficult to do this without melting the grains of gold. Granulation was perfected by Etruscan jewelers and has never been equaled since.

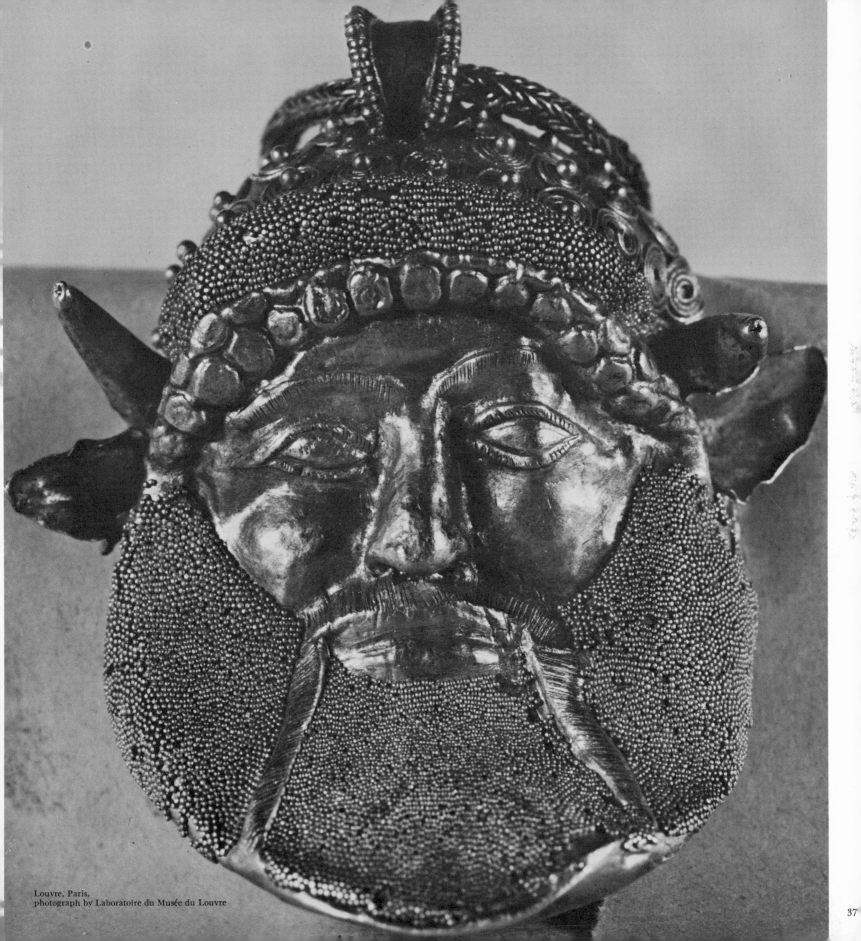

Louvre, Paris,
photograph by Laboratoire du Musée du Louvre

Newark Museum,
photograph by Alfred H. Tamarin

Courtesy, Museum of Fine Arts, Boston, Gift of H. P. Kidder

A large number of Greek clay vases were brought to Italy and buried in Etruscan tombs. Greek pottery-makers also were brought to Italy to work. Etruscan artists copied the magnificent shapes and designs of Greek vases, and as time went on, developed their own style.

The vases were made on the potter's wheel and were beautifully painted. The pitcher on the far left is decorated with an imaginary animal.

A black pottery called *bucchero* was developed by the Etruscans at an early period. The clay pot was shaped and then put into a kiln, a very hot oven, to be fired. The oxygen supply was cut off from the kiln while the pot was being fired; lack of oxygen made the pot turn black. Bucchero ware was unpainted, but the shapes were important.

The bucchero drinking cup on the left is in the shape of a human leg, with a man's face modeled in relief. The bucchero pitcher on the right is in the form of a boy standing on the back of a strange creature.

Vatican Museum,
Alinari-Art Reference Bureau

Many things about the Etruscans are a puzzle to us. We are still not sure who they were, where they came from, what their language meant nor how it sounded. Yet we have a clear picture of them from the art found in their tombs.

Their gay paintings, terracotta statues, bronzes large and small, and beautiful vases, which were in the tombs of the dead, have brought their world to life.

The Etruscans played a very important part in the history of Italy. When the Romans conquered Etruscan cities, they built the foundations of Rome on the Etruscan civilization.

Many of the ways of the Etruscans never really died. They were taken over by the Roman conquerors to become a part of the heritage of Rome, which has been passed on to us.

Satyr carrying off a nymph, bronze, The Metropolitan Museum of Art, Rogers Fund, 1912, photograph by Alfred H. Tamarin

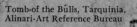
Tomb of the Bulls, Tarquinia,
Alinari-Art Reference Bureau